Vegetarian Ketogenic Cookbook:

30 Delicious and Healthy Vegetarian Recipes for Glowing Skin, Weight Loss And Healthy Life

Table of Contents

Vegetarian Ketogenic Cookbook: 1

30 Delicious and Healthy Vegetarian Recipes for Glowing Skin, Weight Loss And Healthy Life 1

Introduction 3

Chapter 1: Benefits of Vegetarian Ketogenic Diet.....................7

Chapter 2: Delicious Recipes for Breakfast 10

Chapter 3: Amazing Recipes for Lunch...................................20

Chapter 4: Vegetarian Recipes for Dinner 30

Chapter 5: Drink Delicious Smoothies 35

Chapter 6: Delicious Snack Recipes 46

Conclusion 53

Introduction

I want to thank you and congratulate you for downloading the book, *"Vegetarian Ketogenic Cookbook: 30 Delicious and Healthy Vegetarian Recipes for Glowing Skin and Weight Loss"*.

This book contains proven steps and strategies on how to reduce weight and improve your overall health.

Vegetarian diet or veganism is based on the principle that all sentimental people should respect animals. As per vegans, the consumption of any kind of any product is an immoral practice that breaches the premise of vegan diet. With the vulnerable slaughters against animals in the dairy and meat industry, it is easy to see people feel strong about supporting the vegan movement. People are strongly supporting the vegan movement. There is a difference between vegan and vegetarian people. Vegan often keeps them away from all dairy products along with meat, but the vegetarian uses dairy and eggs.

There is no need to worry about fat sources because there are numerous options for your assistance. You can get fat from green and black olives, avocado, coconut oil, red palm oil, olive oil, flaxseed oil, coconut oil, cocoa butter and avocado oil. The vegan protein sources are macadamia nut, unsweetened coconut, pecan, walnut, hazelnut, brazil nut, chia seed, flax seed, tofu, almond flour, almond and pumpkin seed. Dairy is scandalous because some vegetarians include it in their diet and others avoid it. Pastured egg yolks and eggs provide a good amount of healthy fat and are nutrient-dense without carbohydrates.

Unpasteurized (raw) cheese is made from pastured cow milk (the milk of cows that eat grass and provide significant amount of fat without or little carbohydrates) along with overabundance of other nutrients and bacteria for proper bowel. Heavy cream is preferred in the morning coffee because it offers a good amount of fat with little carbohydrates or protein. If you want to follow vegetarian ketogenic diet, you have to set your limitations about dairy products. In this book, you will find numerous recipes to prepare your favorite food.

Thanks again for downloading this book, I hope you enjoy it!

Here is your bonus - Weight Loss Made Easy – <u>Click here to download this ebook</u>

© **Copyright 2017 by Ashley J Williams - All rights reserved.**

This document is geared towards providing exact and reliable information in regards to the topic and issue covered. The publication is sold with the idea that the publisher is not required to render accounting, officially permitted, or otherwise, qualified services. If advice is necessary, legal or professional, a practiced individual in the profession should be ordered.

- From a Declaration of Principles which was accepted and approved equally by a Committee of the American Bar Association and a Committee of Publishers and Associations.

In no way is it legal to reproduce, duplicate, or transmit any part of this document in either electronic means or in printed format. Recording of this publication is strictly prohibited and any storage of this document is not allowed unless with written permission from the publisher. All rights reserved.

The information provided herein is stated to be truthful and consistent, in that any liability, in terms of inattention or otherwise, by any usage or abuse of any policies, processes, or directions contained within is the solitary and utter responsibility of the recipient reader. Under no circumstances will any legal responsibility or blame be held against the publisher for any reparation, damages, or monetary loss due to the information herein, either directly or indirectly.

Respective authors own all copyrights not held by the publisher.

The information herein is offered for informational purposes solely, and is universal as so. The presentation of the information is without contract or any type of guarantee assurance.

The trademarks that are used are without any consent, and the publication of the trademark is without permission or backing by the trademark owner. All trademarks and brands within this book are for clarifying purposes only and are the owned by the owners themselves, not affiliated with this document.

Chapter 1: Benefits of Vegetarian Ketogenic Diet

Ketogenic diet requires you to increase the consumption of fat and restrict the regular consumption of carbohydrates to almost 10 – 15 grams. Regular intake of protein will be 1 gram for one kilogram of your weight. Fish and meat are the main sources of fat; therefore, it is difficult for vegetarians to strictly follow a ketogenic diet. The dairy products, vegetable oils, soy products and eggs are good sources of healthy fat for vegetarians who want to follow a ketogenic diet.

Initially, this diet was used by R.M. Wilders in 1920s for the treatment of pediatric patients. In the presence of anti-seizure medicines, this diet got less attention from public. This diet is now famous for the treatment of epileptic seizes for those patients who can't respond well to standard treatments of anti-seizure. The protein and carbohydrates are the main sources of blood sugar and glucose. If you want to reduce weight, you have to restrict these sources. The diet forces your body to use fat instead of glucose.

Unlike other cells of your body, your brain can't use fat as fuel. When your body have limited glucose, the brain switches it from glucose to ketone bodies. Ketone bodies are the by-product of fat metabolism. It is difficult to turn ketone bodies into energy and this switch in the metabolism causing neurons to build maximum mitochondria or cell engines. Increase in the number of mitochondria is good to give a stabilizing effect to neurons. Ultimately, it prevents the over-excitatory mode of neurons it is a condition that can be the reason of seizures.

Healthy Soy Products

In ketogenic diet, the maximum calories come from protein and fat. As a vegetarian, you will not eat fish or meat, so you should get your protein and fat from other sources. You can use soy products, such as soy beans, soy cheese and soy milk. These are some good sources of fat and protein. Tofu is often used in different meat-tasting dishes, such as tofu is a good substitute for turkey.

Vegetable Oil, Eggs and Dairy

Vegans keep themselves away from every animal product, but the vegetarian can eat eggs and dairy products for protein and fat. To ensure sufficient fat content, select full-fat dairy items, such as full-fat yogurt, milk and cheese. Avoid added sugar because it is an important source of glucose. The eggs have some carbohydrates. You can increase fat content with the use of egg yolk because yolk has more fat than egg white. Vegetable oils are also good to get healthy fat.

Vegan Fat Sources

If you want to get considerable amount of healthy fat from vegan sources, you have to face numerous challenges. To make it easy, you have to turn toward pseudo vegetables, nuts and fruits.

Avocado: It is actually a fruit and provide a healthy amount of monounsaturated fat. It has plethora of nutrients and vitamins, such as fiber is carbohydrate content that feed your bowel bacteria. It will not affect your ketone levels similar to non-fiber carbohydrates.

Coconut: Coconut manna (coconut pulp contains fiber), coconut oil and coconuts provide good amount of saturated fat and medium-chain triglycerides that are easy to turn into ketones.

Macadamia Nuts: These nuts provide the best bang for the culpability in terms of particular fat-to-carbohydrate proportions with 21 grams of healthy fat serving and four grams of carbs.

Almonds: These are the good sources of vitamins and fats, but often lead to different issues because their fat content for each ounce serving drops to almost 14 grams and carbohydrates increase to nearly 6 grams.

In short, you can reduce weight and get all health benefits with the help of vegetarian ketogenic diet. All these substitutes can make your work easy.

Chapter 2: Delicious Recipes for Breakfast

Start your day with healthy vegetarian Ketogenic breakfast. Some recipes are given here to make your work easy in the morning.

Recipe 01: Spinach Omelet

https://sweetandsaucy.files.wordpress.com/2008/06/egg_white_omelet_w_spinach_and_cottage_cheese.jpg

Servings: 1

Total Time: 15 minutes

Ingredients:

- Onion powder: ¼ teaspoon

- Eggs: 2
- Ground nutmeg: 1/8 teaspoon
- Torn Spinach leaves (baby spinach): 1 cup
- Pepper and salt: as per taste
- Parmesan cheese (grated): 1 ½ tablespoons

Instruction:

Whisk eggs in a bowl and mix in parmesan cheese and baby spinach. Season with pepper, salt, nutmeg, and onion powder.

Grease one small skillet with olive oil or cooking spray over medium flame. Cook egg mixture for almost 3 minutes, until moderately set.

Flip egg with one spatula and continue cooking 2 – 3 minutes. Decrease heat to almost low and continue cooking again for 2 – 3 minutes. Serve hot.

Nutrition Value:

Calories: 186 kcal, Carbs: 2.8 g, Fat: 12.3 g, Protein: 16.4 g, Cholesterol: 379 mg, Sodium: 279 mg.

Recipe 02: Spinach Quiche

http://www.onceuponachef.com/images/2010/09/Spinach-Quiche.jpg

Servings: 6

Total Time: 50 minutes

Ingredients:

- Vegetable oil: 1 tablespoon
- Muenster cheese (shredded): 3 cups
- Salt: ¼ teaspoon
- Chopped onion: 1
- Black pepper (ground): 1/8 teaspoon

- Chopped spinach (frozen, drained and thawed): 10 ounces
- Whisked eggs: 5

Instruction:

Preheat your oven to almost 350 °F. Grease one 9-inch pie pan.

Heat some oil in a skillet over medium flame. Cook onions in the skillet and stir occasionally, until onions become soft. Mix in spinach and cook well to evaporate extra moisture.

Take one large bowl and combine pepper, salt, cheese and eggs in this bowl. Now add spinach blend and mix well. Scoop in your greased pie pan.

Now bake in your preheated oven for almost 30 minutes. Let it cool for almost 10 minutes and serve.

Nutrition Value:

Calories: 309 kcal, Carbs: 4.8 g, Fat: 23.7 g, Protein: 20.4 g, Cholesterol: 209 mg, Sodium: 546 mg.

Recipe 03: Spinach Brownies

http://img.sndimg.com/food/image/upload/h_465,w_620,c_fit/v1/img/recipes/60/91/1/pic1zqhwV.jpg

Servings: 24

Total Time: 55 minutes

Ingredients:

- Chopped and rinsed spinach: 10 ounces
- Milk: 1 cup
- Melted butter: ½ cup
- All-purpose flour: 1 cup
- Chopped onion: 1
- Salt: 1 teaspoon
- Mozzarella cheese (shredded): 8 ounces
- Baking powder: 1 teaspoon
- Eggs: 2

Instruction:

Preheat your oven to almost 375 °F. Grease a baking dish (9x13-inch).

Put spinach in one medium saucepan with sufficient water to cover spinach. Let it boil and decrease heat to simmer. Cook for almost 3 minutes to limp spinach. Turn off heat. Drain spinach and keep it aside.

Take one large bowl and mix baking powder, salt and flour. Mix in butter, milk and eggs. Stir in mozzarella cheese, onion and spinach.

Transfer this mixture to your greased baking dish. Bake in your preheated oven for almost 30 – 35 minutes. Check with a toothpick, if it comes out clean, the brownies are ready.

Nutrition Value:

Calories: 92 kcal, Carbs: 5.6 g, Fat: 6 g, Protein: 4.1 g, Cholesterol: 32 mg, Sodium: 216 mg.

Recipe 04: Vegan Muffin

Servings: 12

Total Time: 45 minutes

Ingredients:

- Ripe bananas: 3
- Maple syrup: 1/2 cup
- Canola oil: 3 tablespoons
- Spelt flour: 1 1/2 cups
- Baking soda: 1 1/2 teaspoons
- Salt: 1/4 teaspoon
- Pecans: 3/4 cup

Instructions:

Preheat your oven to almost 350°F. Grease your muffin tins.

Take one bowl and mash bananas and mix in vanilla, canola oil and maple syrup.

Take another bowl and sift all dry ingredients together. Blend them with banana mixture and mix them well. Add pecans in the last and toss this mixture.

Pour into muffin tins and bake for almost 42 minutes. Check with a toothpick and serve.

Nutrition Value:

Calories: 451 kcal, Carbs: 59.2 g, Fat: 23.2 g, Protein: 4.1 g, Cholesterol: 0 mg, Sodium: 386 mg.

Recipe 05: Cauliflower Pizza

http://us.naturespath.com/sites/default/files/recipe/20150512/cauliflower_pizza_crust-low-res.jpg

Servings: 4

Total Time: 1 hour

Ingredients:

- Parmigiano-Reggiano cheese (grated): ½ ounce
- Separated and cored cauliflower: 1 head
- Egg: 1 large
- Water: ½ cup

- Cayenne pepper: 1 pinch
- Salt: ½ teaspoon
- Goat cheese: 2 ounces

Instruction:

Preheat your oven to almost 400 °F. Line one baking sheet with baking/parchment paper.

Use your food processor to puree cauliflower to make it finely ground.

Cook salt, water and ground cauliflower together in one skillet over medium flame for almost 5 – 6 minutes to evaporate water. Let it completely cool.

Transfer cauliflower mixture to the middle of one clean dish towel. Squeeze and wrap tightly to remove extra moisture. You will have almost 1 ½ cups cauliflower pulp.

Stir cayenne pepper, egg, parmigiana-reggiano cheese, goat cheese and cauliflower in one bowl to make a soft dough. Gather this dough to make a ball and put in the middle of greased baking sheet. Press dough in the middle to make ¼-inch thick circle.

Bake it in your preheated oven for almost 40 minutes to make it golden brown. Let it cool and turn this crust over before using your favorite topping.

Nutrition Value:

Calories: 121 kcal, Carbs: 8.2 g, Fat: 6.6 g, Protein: 8.8 g, Cholesterol: 61 mg, Sodium: 479 mg.

Recipe 06: Cauliflower Rice

Servings: 6

Total Time: 45 minutes

Ingredients:

- Cubed carrot: 1 large
- Frozen peas: 2 cups
- Minced garlic: 2 cloves
- Water: ½ cup
- Shredded cauliflower: 20 ounces
- Sesame oil (divided): ¼ cup
- Soy sauce: 6 tablespoons
- Whisked eggs: 2
- Sliced green onions: 6

Instruction:

Stir water and peas together in one saucepan and let it boil. Decrease heat to medium and cook for almost 5 minutes to tender peas. Drain and dispose of water.

Heat two tablespoons sesame oil in one wok over medium heat. Sauté garlic, carrot and onions in hot oil for almost 5 minutes to make them soft. Now add cauliflower, cook and mix until the cauliflower becomes tender. It will take almost 4 – 5 minutes.

Stir soy sauce and peas in cauliflower mixture and stir-fry this mixture for almost 3 – 5 minutes.

Move this mixture to side of wok and pour whisked eggs on empty side. Quickly scramble eggs for almost 3 – 5 minutes until heated through. Mix cooked eggs in cauliflower mixture and break up large chunks. Serve hot.

Nutrition Value:

Calories: 366 kcal, Carbs: 15.8 g, Fat: 19.2 g, Protein: 33.3 g, Cholesterol: 132 mg, Sodium: 1065 mg.

Chapter 3: Amazing Recipes for Lunch

If you want something healthy in your lunch, here are some delicious recipes with easy instructions.

Recipe 07: Jalapeno Poppers

Servings: 32

Total Time: 1 hour

Ingredients:

- Softened cream cheese: 12 ounces
- Milk: 1 cup
- All-purpose flour: 1 cup
- Cheddar cheese (shredded): 8 ounces
- Bread crumbs (dry): 1 cup
- Bacon bits: 1 tablespoon

- Jalapeno peppers (halved and seeded): 12 ounces
- Frying oil: 2 quarts

Instruction:

Take one medium bowl and mix bacon bits, cheddar cheese and cream cheese in this bowl. Spoon this blend in the halves of jalapeno pepper.

Put flour and milk into two separate bowls. Dip the stuffed jalapeno spices in milk and then flour. Coat them well and keep them aside for almost 10 minutes.

Dip jalapeno peppers in the milk again and roll them in the breadcrumbs. Let them dry and repeat to coat entire surface of jalapeno.

Take one medium skillet and heat oil to almost 365 °F. Deep fry all coated jalapenos for 2 – 3 minutes to make them golden brown. Drain friend jalapeno peppers on one paper towel. Serve hot with your favorite sauce.

Nutrition Value:

Calories: 149 kcal, Carbs: 6.8 g, Fat: 12 g, Protein: 3.9 g, Cholesterol: 20 mg, Sodium: 110 mg.

Recipe 08: Zucchini Pasta

Servings: 1

Total Time: 15 minutes

Ingredients:

- Water: ¼ cup
- Peeled zucchinis: 2
- Black pepper (ground) and salt: as per taste
- Olive oil: 1 tablespoon

Instruction:

Cut lengthways slices from a zucchini with the help of one vegetable peeler. Stop peeling as you reach seeds.

Flip zucchini over and keep peeling until you get long strips of whole zucchini. Discard seeds. Turn zucchini in thin strips that look similar to spaghetti.

Take skillet to heat olive oil over medium flame and cook zucchini in hot oil for almost 1 minute. Add some water and cook for almost 5 – 7 minutes to make zucchini soft. Season with pepper and salt.

Nutrition Value:

Calories: 157 kcal, Carbs: 7.9 g, Fat: 13.9 g, Protein: 2.9 g, Cholesterol: 0 mg, Sodium: 181 mg.

Recipe 09: Asparagus and Mushrooms

Total Time: 25 minutes

Servings: 6

Ingredients:

- Fresh asparagus (trimmed): 1 bunch
- Fresh mushrooms (quartered): ½ pound
- Minced rosemary: 2 sprigs
- Olive oil: 2 teaspoons
- Salt as per taste

- Ground pepper (black): as per taste

Instructions:

Preheat your oven at almost 450 °F. Grease one cookie sheet with cooking spray. Keep it aside.

Take one bowl and add mushrooms and asparagus in this bowl. Sprinkle olive oil, salt, pepper and rosemary on asparagus.

Mix all ingredients well and spread these mixtures on cookie sheet. Roast this blend in a preheated oven for almost 15 minutes. Serve hot.

Nutrition Value:

Calories: 38 kcal, Carbs: 4.3 g, Fat: 1.8 g, Protein: 2.8 g, Cholesterol: 0 mg, Sodium: 84 mg.

Recipe 10: Asparagus Soup

Total Time: 30 minutes

Servings: 4

Ingredients:

- Butter: 25g
- Vegetable Oil: a little
- Asparagus spear (discard woody ends and chop stalks and tips, keep tips separate): 350g
- Shallow (Fine slices): 3
- Crushed garlic: 2 cloves
- Spinach: 2 handfuls
- Vegetable stock: 700ml
- Olive oil to drizzle
- Rustic bread: to serve

Instructions:

Take one large saucepan and heat oil and butter in this pan. Fry tips of asparagus for a few minutes to make them soft. Transfer them to a plate and keep it aside.

Add asparagus stalks, garlic and shallots in similar pan and cook for almost 10 minutes. Mix in spinach and stock. Let them boil and blitz with one hand blender.

Sprinkle pepper and salt and pour hot water as per your need. Ladle this blend into bowls and sprinkle asparagus tips in each bowl. Drizzle with oil and serve with rustic bread.

Nutrition Value:

Calories: 196 kcal, Carbs: 14.1 g, Fat: 13.4 g, Protein: 6.6 g, Cholesterol: 35 mg, Sodium: 1101 mg.

Recipe 11: Zucchini Pasta with Asparagus

http://dishingupthedirt.com/wp-content/uploads/2014/06/Garlic-Scape-pesto-and-Zuchhini-Pasta3.jpg

Total Time: 30 minutes

Servings: 8

Ingredients:

- Zucchini Pasta: 16 ounce
- Dry dill weed: 1 teaspoon
- Black pepper (ground): as per taste
- Olive oil (extra virgin and divided): ¼ cup
- Avocadoes (pitted, peeled and mashed): 2
- Minced garlic: 2 cloves
- Trimmed asparagus spears (chopped): 1 pound
- Grape tomatoes (halved): 2 cups
- Vegetable broth: 14.5 ounce
- Lime juice: ½ lime
- Garlic powder: ½ teaspoon

- Shredded Mexican cheese: 1 cup

Instructions:

Shred zucchini to make pasta and keep it aside (follow recipe 08)

Heat leftover oil (3 tablespoons) in one skillet on medium heat and cook garlic for 2 minutes. Add tomatoes, and asparagus and mix well to coat and pour broth in this skillet. Continue cooking without covering this skillet for almost ten minutes or to tender asparagus.

Put the pasta in one large bowl and toss with tomato and asparagus mixture. Sprinkle with pepper and dill. Take a separate bowl to mix lime juice, garlic powder and avocados, until blended.

Now serve pasta with one dollop of avocado mixture and top with cheese (shredded).

Nutrition Value:

Calories: 95 kcal, Carbs: 2.2 g, Fat: 3.1 g, Protein: 7.5 g, Cholesterol: 68 mg, Sodium: 255 mg.

Recipe 12: Pan Fried Asparagus

Servings: 4

Total Time: 25 minutes

Ingredients:

- Butter: ¼ cup
- Black pepper (ground): ¼ teaspoon
- Olive oil: 2 tablespoons
- Minced garlic: 3 cloves
- Trimmed asparagus spears: 1 pound
- Coarse salt: 1 teaspoon

Instruction:

Melt butter in the skillet over medium heat. Mix in pepper, salt and olive oil. Cook garlic in melted butter for one minute, but avoid overcooking.

Add asparagus and cook this blend for almost 10 minutes, turn asparagus for even cooking. Serve hot.

Nutrition Value:

Calories: 188 kcal, Carbs: 5.2 g, Fat: 18.4 g, Protein: 2.8 g, Cholesterol: 31 mg, Sodium: 525 mg.

Chapter 4: Vegetarian Recipes for Dinner

Your dinner should be free from unhealthy ingredients; therefore, you can try these healthy recipes.

Recipe 13: Mushroom and Asparagus Pastry Pie

Total Time: 1 hour

Servings: 8

Ingredients:

- Butter: ½ cup
- Asparagus (trimmed and 1" pieces): 2 bunches
- Fresh mushrooms (sliced): 1 pound
- Hollandaise sauce: 1 cup
- Diced garlic: 6 cloves
- Puff pastry (thawed, gluten-free): 17.25 ounce

Instructions:

Preheat an oven to almost 400 °F.

Take a skillet and melt butter in this skillet on medium heat. Cook asparagus in this skillet for almost 10 minutes. Mix in garlic and mushrooms. Cook and mix to tender mushrooms. Keep it aside.

Prepare your hollandaise sauce as per the instructions given on the package. Mix this sauce with mushrooms and asparagus.

Put one sheet of your puff pastry in the base of one 9x13" baking dish. Adjust extra dough to its sides and spread asparagus mixture equally over dough. Top with other pastry sheet and pinch the edges to seal all ingredients.

It is time to bake the pastry for almost 30 minutes in your preheated oven to make pastry golden brown. Slice before serving.

Nutrition Value:

Calories: 121 kcal, Carbs: 6.5 g, Fat: 8.4 g, Protein: 10.9 g, Cholesterol: 78 mg, Sodium: 913 mg.

Recipe 14: Pumpkin Soup

Servings: 4

Preparation Time: 30 to 45 minutes

Ingredients:

- Olive oil: 1 Tablespoons
- Chopped onions: 2 cups
- Whole wheat flour: 2 teaspoons
- Vegetable stock (reduced fat and sodium): 4 cups
- Pumpkin purée: 3 cups (puree pumpkin in blender)
- Minced garlic: ½ teaspoon
- Black beans: ½ can
- Ground cumin: ½ teaspoon
- Salt: ¼ teaspoon
- Powdered white pepper: ¼ teaspoon
- Grated nutmeg: Dusting

Instructions:

Caramelize chopped onion in some olive oil over medium heat in a skillet. Sprinkle flour over this mixture and cook for almost two minutes to make this mixture slightly thick.

Mix in salt, pepper, cumin, garlic, pumpkin and broth. Whisk well and let this soup simmer for almost 15 minutes over medium flame.

Stir occasionally to avoid scorching. Mix beans in this soup and cook for nearly 15 minutes again. Stir occasionally and serve hot. You can use blender to puree this soup.

Nutrition Value:

Calories: 99 kcal, Carbs: 5.5 g, Fat: 5.9 g, Protein: 7.9 g, Cholesterol: 45 mg, Sodium: 952 mg.

Recipe 15: Apple and Peach Salsa

Total Time: 3 hours 20 minutes

Servings: 6

Ingredients:

- Diced peaches: 1 cup
- Diced apple: 1/2 cup
- Diced avocado: 1/2 cup
- Diced tomato: 1/2 cup
- Green onion (Chopped): 1/3 cup
- Chopped cilantro: 1/4 cup
- Lemon juice: 2 tablespoons
- Olive oil: 2 tablespoons
- Sesame oil (toasted): 1 teaspoon
- Ground cumin: 1 teaspoon
- Jalapeno pepper (seeded & minced): 1
- Black pepper (ground) and salt: as per taste

Instructions:

Take one bowl and mix jalapeno pepper, black pepper, salt, cumin, sesame oil, olive oil, lemon juice, cilantro, green onion, tomato, avocado, apple and peaches in this bowl.

Cover this bowl with one plastic wrap and put in your fridge for almost three hours to blend all flavors. Serve this salsa chilled.

Nutrition Value:

Calories: 78 kcal, Carbs: 4.5 g, Fat: 1.4 g, Protein: 9.9 g, Cholesterol: 0 mg, Sodium: 256 mg.

Chapter 5: Drink Delicious Smoothies

You can start your day with delicious smoothies that are healthy and full of nutrients.

Recipe 16: Peach Smoothie

Servings: 1 to 2

Preparation Time: 5 minutes

Ingredients:

- Rinsed kale: 1 to 2 handfuls
- Peach: 1 pitted
- Banana: 1
- Strawberries: 1 handful
- Flax seeds: 1/8 cup
- Goji berries: 1/8 cup

- Water

Instructions:

Add all fruits and vegetables in a blender and add water to Max Line and extract all nutrients. You can enjoy a glass of extract nutrients with some ice.

Nutrition Value:

Recipe 17: Green Smoothie

Servings: 1 to 2

Preparation Time: 5 minutes

Ingredients:

- Swiss chard (rinsed): 1 to 2 handfuls
- Apricot: 1
- Cored pineapple: 1 cup
- Apple: 1
- Blueberries: 1 cup
- Goji berries (soaked): ¼ cup
- Water

Instructions:

Add all fruits and vegetables in blender and add water to Max Line and extract all nutrients. You can enjoy a glass of extract nutrients with some ice.

Nutrition Value:

Calories: 204 kcal, Carbs: 48.5 g, Fat: 0.5 g, Protein: 4.3 g, Cholesterol: 2 mg, Sodium: 34 mg.

Recipe 18: Pineapple Smoothie

Servings: 1 to 2

Preparation Time: 5 minutes

Ingredients:

- Collard greens (rinsed): 1 to 2 handfuls
- Banana: 1
- Pineapple: 1 cup
- Red grapes: 1 cup
- Hemp seeds: ¼ cup
- Water

Instructions:

Add all fruits and vegetables in blender and add water to Max Line and extract all nutrients. You can enjoy a glass of extract nutrients with some ice.

Nutrition Value

Calories: 235 kcal, Carbs: 38.5 g, Fat: 1.5 g, Protein: 20.3 g, Cholesterol: 0 mg, Sodium: 143 mg.

Recipe 19: Grapes and Beet Smoothie

Servings: 1 to 2

Preparation Time: 5 minutes

Ingredients:

- Raw beet: ¼
- Red grapes without seeds: 10
- Broccoli florets: 2 small
- Raspberries: 10
- Goji berries: 1 tablespoon
- Small avocado (peeled and pitted): ½
- Olive oil: 1 teaspoon

Instructions:

Add all fruits, olive oil and vegetables in blender and add water to Max Line and extract all nutrients. You can enjoy a glass of extract nutrients with some ice.

Nutrition Value:

Calories: 256 kcal, Carbs: 41.5 g, Fat: 0.7 g, Protein: 3.3 g, Cholesterol: 1 mg, Sodium: 32 mg.

Recipe 20: Cholesterol Enemy

Servings: 1 to 2

Preparation Time: 5 minutes

Ingredients:

- Kale: 2 handfuls
- Blueberries: 1 cup
- Banana: ½
- Cooked oatmeal: ⅓ cup
- Almonds: 10
- Raw cacao: 2 tablespoons

Instructions:

Add all fruits, nuts and vegetables in blender and add water to Max Line and extract all nutrients. You can enjoy a glass of extract nutrients with some ice.

Nutrition Value:

Calories: 261 kcal, Carbs: 38.5 g, Fat: 1.5 g, Protein: 9.3 g, Cholesterol: 0 mg, Sodium: 39 mg.

Recipe 21: Chocolate Milk

Cooking Time: 5 minutes

Servings: 2 servings

Ingredients:

- Almond milk (unsweetened): 16 ounces
- Low-carb sweetener: to taste
- Heavy cream: 4 ounces
- Whey chocolate powder: 1 scoop
- Crushed ice: ½ cup

Instructions:

Put all above mentioned ingredients in your blender and blend them well to make a smooth paste. Serve chilled.

Nutrition: Calories: 292, Fat: 25 grams, Carbs: 5 and Protein: 15 grams

Recipe 22: Chocolate Smoothie

Cooking Time: 10 minutes

Servings: 2 to 4

Ingredients:

- 2/3 cups berries
- Whey protein, 1 scoop
- ¼ cup water
- 1 cup chocolate milk
- 2 egg yolks, raw only

Instructions:

It is very simple, just take a full-size cup, blend all the ingredients and add crushed ice. You are done to enjoy your favorite chocolate bombs.

Nutrition Value:

279 total calories, 5.4 g fat, 9.7 g protein, 50.6 g carbohydrate, 122 mg sodium, 20 mg cholesterol

Recipe 23: Strawberry Smoothie

Cooking Time: 5 to 10 minutes

Servings: 2

Ingredients:

- Almond milk, 1 cup
- 2 tablespoons crushed almonds
- 1/3 cup strawberries
- One pinches salt

Instructions:

Take a food processor and make a blend of all these ingredients to make a delicious smoothie. Serve chilled by keeping in the refrigerator.

Nutritional Information:

840 total calories, 70 g fat, 27 g protein, 27 g carbohydrate and 2 g fiber.

Recipe 24: Blueberry Smoothie

Cooking Time: 10 minutes

Servings: 2

Ingredients:

- Almond milk, 1 cup
- 2 tablespoons crushed almonds
- 1/3 cup blueberries or any other berries of your choice
- One pinch salt

Instructions:

Take a food processor and make a blend of all these ingredients to make a delicious smoothie. Serve chilled by keeping in the refrigerator.

Nutritional Value:

835 total calories, 80 g fat, 30 g protein, 27 g carbohydrate and 2 g fiber.

Chapter 6: Delicious Snack Recipes

Recipe 25: Zucchini Fries

https://www.twopeasandtheirpod.com/wp-content/uploads/2010/12/baked-zucchini-fries.jpg

Servings: 6

Total Time: 1 hour 55 minutes

Ingredients:

- Ground almonds: ½ cup
- Zucchini: 2
- Parmesan cheese (grated): ½ cup
- Salt: 1 tablespoon
- Italian herb dried seasoning: ½ teaspoon
- Eggs: 2

Instruction:

Preheat your oven to almost 425 °F. Line one baking sheet with baking/parchment paper.

Slice zucchini into 3-inch long pieces and cut 9 fries from each piece. Put these fries into one colander and sprinkle some salt. Keep it aside for almost one hour to drain zucchini pieces and remove extra liquid.

Whisk eggs in one shallow bowl. Mix Italian seasoning, parmesan cheese and almond in another shallow bowl. Rinse zucchini to remove salt and pat zucchini pieces, to make them dry, with some paper towels.

Dip every zucchini piece in whisked egg and roll in the almond coating. Put coated fries on greased baking sheet.

Bake in your preheated oven for almost 25 minutes to make zucchini crispy and brown. Turn them halfway while cooking. Serve hot with your favorite sauce.

Nutrition Value:

Calories: 98 kcal, Carbs: 4.5 g, Fat: 5.4 g, Carbs: 4.5 g, Protein: 8.9 g, Cholesterol: 68 mg, Sodium: 1293 mg.

Recipe 26: Avocado Salsa

Total Time: 25 minutes

Servings: 16

Ingredients:

- Corn kernels: 2 cups
- Avocado (pitted, diced and chopped): 2 cups
- Red onion (diced): 1 cup
- White onion (diced): 1 cup
- Red bell pepper (diced): 1 cup
- Green bell pepper (diced): 1/2 cup
- Olive oil: 1/4 cup
- White vinegar: 2 tablespoons
- Salt: 1 1/2 tablespoons
- Ground cumin: 2 teaspoons
- Black pepper (ground): 2 teaspoons
- Red vinegar: 1 teaspoon
- Chili powder: 1 teaspoon
- Cilantro leaves (chopped): 2 cups

- Diced tomatoes: 1 1/2 cups
- Juiced and zested: 1 lime

Instructions:

Heat oil in one skillet over high flame and cook corn kernel in your hot skillet. Turn frequently to avoid burning. You have to cook for almost five minutes.

Take one mixing bowl and mix corn, chili powder, red vinegar, black pepper, cumin, salt, white vinegar, olive oil, bell pepper (green) and bell pepper (red), white onion, red onion and avocado in this bowl. Add tomatoes, lime juice, lime zest and cilantro to corn mixture and stir gently to incorporate all ingredients.

Nutrition Value:

Calories: 101 kcal, Carbs: 8.5 g, Fat: 2.4 g, Protein: 8.9 g, Cholesterol: 68 mg, Sodium: 650 mg.

Recipe 27: Stuffed Avocado

Total Time: 30 minutes

Servings: 6

Ingredients:

- Poblano pepper: 1 chopped
- Tomato: 1 chopped
- Lime: 1
- Sea salt: ¼ teaspoon
- Chopped onion: ½
- Chopped cilantro: 3 tablespoons
- Cayenne pepper: ¼ teaspoon

- Avocados (pitted & halved): 4

Instructions:

Take a medium bowl and mix pepper, tomato, onion, cilantro and salt. Take one spoon of the mixture and keep it in the avocado half.

You can scoop out some pulp to put in the salsa. Sprinkle lime juice over it and serve. You can use baked vegetables in salsa as well.

Nutrition Value:

Calories: 265 kcal, Carbs: 9.5 g, Fat: 15.4 g, Protein: 11.9 g, Cholesterol: 69 mg, Sodium: 993 mg.

Recipe 28: Mushroom Sauce

Total Time: 30 minutes

Servings: 8

Ingredients:

- Vegetable broth: 2 cups
- Green onions (chopped): ½ cup
- All-purpose flour: ½ cup
- Soy Butter: ½ cup
- Diced mushrooms: ¾ pound

Instructions:

Take one medium saucepan and put it on medium heat. Combine green onions, flour, broth, butter and mushrooms in this pan.

Cook well and stir constantly to make it thick and golden brown. Serve this sauce with grilled food.

Nutrition Value:

Calories: 198 kcal, Carbs: 14.5 g, Fat: 12.4 g, Protein: 14.9 g, Cholesterol: 2.5 mg, Sodium: 893 mg.

Recipe 29: Vegan Dip

Total Time: 30 minutes

Servings: 12

Ingredients:

- Mushrooms: 1 pint
- Tahini: 2 teaspoons
- Salt: ¼ teaspoon
- Chopped walnuts: 2 ounces
- Black pepper (ground): ¼ teaspoon
- Vegan Mayonnaise: 3 tablespoons
- Bread rounds (pita): 2
- Chopped garlic: 1 tablespoon

Instructions:

Use one food processor to chop all mushrooms and transfer them to one bowl.

Mix in salt, pepper, tahini, garlic, walnuts and mayonnaise along with mushrooms to equally combine each and everything. Serve this dip along pita bread.

Nutrition Value:

Calories: 108 kcal, Carbs: 9.5 g, Fat: 15.4 g, Protein: 81.9 g, Cholesterol: 68 mg, Sodium: 793 mg.

Recipe 30: Fruit Salad

Cooking Time: 10 minutes

Servings: 2

Ingredients:

- 1 cup berries (you can prepare a mixture by selecting your own favorite berries)
- 2 tablespoons mascarpone
- 1 sage leaf, small pieces
- 1/2 vanilla bean
- 1/2 tablespoons cream (heavy or whipping cream)

Instructions:

Take a bowl to prepare a mixture of berries and cut sage. In a separate bowl, make the mixture of rest of the ingredients and then keep in the microwave for 10 seconds. Mix the blend of both the bowls and enjoy chilled.

Nutrition Value

1.5 g fat, 4 g carbohydrate, and 2 g fiber.

Conclusion

The vegetarian diet is an ultimate diet for fat loss and ethical consumption. In contrast, the traditional diet includes the heavy intake of animal fats. It is considered that the ketogenic diet and vegan diet are two different sides of a coin. A traditional vegan diet is designed on the basis of high carb-to-fat macronutrient ratio. On the other hand, the ketogenic diet needs a particular fat-to-carb macronutrient proportion.

In this situation, dieters often think about the fat-burning benefits of nutritious ketosis while abiding by the moral principles of veganism. Is there anything like vegetarian ketogenic diet? The answer is yes because the macronutrient proportion of the Keto diet is inflexible because lots of calories should come from fat with few soluble carbohydrates (limited to 20 grams per day). The use of animal products with vegan diet is non-negotiable; therefore, all dairy and meat should be avoided.

Thank you again for downloading this book!

I hope this book was able to help you to improve your overall health.

Finally, if you enjoyed this book, then I'd like to ask you for a favor, would you be kind enough to leave a review for this book on Amazon? It'd be greatly appreciated!

Click here to leave a review for this book on Amazon!

Thank you and good luck!

Made in the USA
Middletown, DE
09 October 2017